Seven Wonders of
ANCIENT
NORTH AMERICA

Michael Woods and Mary B. Woods

TWENTY-FIRST CENTURY BOOKS

Minneapolis

To the Rockefeller Foundation Bellagio Center

PHOTO ACKNOWLEDGMENTS

The images in this book are used with the permission of: © All Canada Photos/Alamy, p. 6; © Laura Westlund/Independent Picture Service, pp. 7, 15, 25, 35, 45, 55, 63; © Bridgeman Art Library, London/SuperStock, p. 8; © Bettmann/CORBIS, p. 9; © Hulton Archive/Getty Images, p. 10; The Art Archive/Prehistoric Museum Moesgard Højbjerg Denmark/Gianni Dagli Orti, p. 12; © George Hunter/SuperStock, p. 13 (top); © David Muenker/Alamy, p. 13 (bottom); © SuperStock, Inc./SuperStock, pp. 14, 69 (top); © North Wind Picture Archives, pp. 16, 18, 21, 31, 38, 40, 62, 65 (top), 68; © Philip Scalia/Alamy, p. 17 (top); © Stock Montage, Inc./Alamy, p. 17 (bottom); © MPI/Hulton Archive/Getty Images, p. 20; © George Catlin/The Bridgeman Art Library/Getty Images, pp. 22, 72 (top right); © Raymond K. Gehman/National Geographic/Getty Images, p. 23 (both); Cahokia Mounds State Historic Site, pp. 24, 27 (top); Michael Hampshire, Cahokia Mounds State Historic Site, pp. 26, 30; © Southern Illinois University/AFP/Getty Images, pp. 27 (bottom), 72 (bottom right); William R. Iseminger, Cahokia Mounds State Historic Site, p. 28; Lloyd K. Townsend, Cahokia Mounds State Historic Site, p. 29; © Don Smetzer/Alamy, p. 32; © Ernest Manewal/SuperStock, p. 34; The Denver Public Library, Western History Collection, Thomas Michael McKee, Z-1442, p. 36; The Denver Public Library, Western History Collection, William Henry Jackson, WHJ-1241, p. 37; © Karlene Schwartz, p. 39 (top); © Witold Skrypczak/SuperStock, p. 39 (bottom); © Wil Meinderts/Foto Natura/Minden Pictures/Getty Images, p. 41 (top); © age fotostock/SuperStock, pp. 41 (bottom), 53 (bottom), 54, 59, 71; The Denver Public Library, Western History Collection, George L. Beam, GB-8439, p. 42; © Prisma/SuperStock, p. 43; © Danny Lehman/CORBIS, p. 44; Universidad Nacional Autónoma de México, Instituto de Investigaciones Filológicas, Centro de Estudios Mayas, México, p. 46; Photographs by Linda Schele, © David Schele, courtesy Foundation for the Advancement of Mesoamerican Studies, Inc., www.famsi.org, pp. 47, 50; © Werner Forman/Art Resource, NY, pp. 48, 66; © Peter M. Wilson/Alamy, p. 49; © Kenneth Garrett/Woodfin Camp/Time & Life Pictures/Getty Images, p. 51; © Kenneth Garrett/National Geographic/Getty Images, p. 53 (top); © Mark Newman/SuperStock, p. 56; © A.A.M. Van der Heyden/Independent Picture Service, p. 57 (both); © R. H. Productions/Robert Harding World Imagery/Getty Images, p. 60; © Luis Acosta/AFP/Getty Images, p. 61; © Schalkwijk/Art Resource, NY, p. 64; © Classic Image/Alamy, p. 65 (bottom); © DEA/G. Dagli Orti/De Agostini Picture Library/Getty Images, p. 67; © Image Asset Management Ltd./SuperStock, p. 69 (bottom); © David McLain/Aurora/Getty Images, p. 72 (top left); © Roger Viollet Collection/Getty Images, p. 72 (middle left); © Vladimir Pcholkin/Taxi/Getty Images, p. 72 (middle right); © Tom Till/Photographer's Choice/Getty Images, p. 72 (bottom left); © Spanish School/The Bridgeman Art Library/Getty Images, p. 72 (bottom middle).

Front Cover: © George Catlin/The Bridgeman Art Library/Getty Images (top left); © David McLain/Aurora/Getty Images (top middle); © Roger Viollet Collection/Getty Images (top right); © Tom Till/Photographer's Choice/Getty Images (middle); © Spanish School/The Bridgeman Art Library/Getty Images (bottom left); © Vladimir Pcholkin/Taxi/Getty Images (bottom middle); © Southern Illinois University/AFP/Getty Images (bottom right).

Twenty-First Century Books
A division of Lerner Publishing Group, Inc.
241 First Avenue North
Minneapolis, MN 55401 U.S.A.

Website address: www.lernerbooks.com

Library of Congress Cataloging-in-Publication Data

Woods, Mary B. (Mary Boyle), 1946–
   The Seven Wonders of Ancient North America / by Mary B. Woods and Michael Woods.
      p.   cm. — (Seven wonders)
   Includes bibliographical references and index.
   ISBN-13: 978-0-8225-7572-6 (lib. bdg. : alk. paper)
   1. Indians of North America—Antiquities—Juvenile literature. 2. Indians of Mexico—Antiquities—Juvenile literature. 3. North America—Antiquities—Juvenile literature. 4. Mexico—Antiquities—Juvenile literature. I. Woods, Michael, 1946– II. Title.
   E77.4.W69 2009
   970.01—dc22   2007037236

Manufactured in the United States of America
1 2 3 4 5 6 – DP – 14 13 12 11 10 09

Contents

INTRODUCTION

*P*EOPLE LOVE TO MAKE LISTS OF THE BIGGEST AND THE BEST. ALMOST 2,500 YEARS AGO, A GREEK WRITER MADE A LIST OF THE MOST AWESOME THINGS EVER BUILT. THE LIST INCLUDED BUILDINGS, STATUES, AND OTHER OBJECTS THAT WERE LARGE, WONDROUS, AND IMPRESSIVE. OTHER ANCIENT WRITERS ADDED THEIR OWN IDEAS TO THE LIST. WRITERS EVENTUALLY AGREED ON A FINAL LIST. IT WAS CALLED THE SEVEN WONDERS OF THE ANCIENT WORLD. THE ANCIENT WONDERS WERE:

THE GREAT PYRAMID AT GIZA: *a tomb for an ancient Egyptian king. The pyramid still stands in Giza, Egypt.*

THE COLOSSUS OF RHODES: *a giant bronze statue of Helios, the Greek sun god. The statue stood in Rhodes, an island in the Aegean Sea.*

THE LIGHTHOUSE OF ALEXANDRIA: *an enormous lighthouse. It stood in the harbor in Alexandria, Egypt.*

THE HANGING GARDENS OF BABYLON: *magnificent gardens in the ancient city of Babylon (near modern-day Baghdad, Iraq)*

THE MAUSOLEUM AT HALICARNASSUS: *a marble tomb for a ruler in the Persian Empire. It was located in the ancient city of Halicarnassus (in modern Turkey).*

THE STATUE OF ZEUS AT OLYMPIA: *a statue honoring the king of the Greek gods. It stood in Olympia, Greece.*

THE TEMPLE OF ARTEMIS AT EPHESUS: *a temple honoring a Greek goddess. It stood on the coast of the Aegean Sea, in modern-day Turkey.*

Most of these ancient wonders are no longer standing. They were destroyed by wars, earthquakes, weather, and the passage of time.

Over the years, people made other lists of wonders. They listed wonders of the modern world and wonders of the natural world. They even listed wonders for each continent on Earth. This book is about ancient wonders from the continent of North America.

A WONDROUS PLACE

The huge area of land that is North America is the third-largest of Earth's seven continents. North America includes the United States, Canada, Mexico, the Caribbean Islands, and Greenland.

Earth was in an ice age from eighty thousand to twelve thousand years ago. The weather was so cold that snow fell and never melted. Thick ice covered Canada and the northern United States. The ice made it possible for ancient people to move to North America. They probably began arriving in North America about forty thousand years ago.

They built villages and cities long before European explorers arrived. Ancient people developed their own cultures, or ways of life. As you will discover in this book, some of these people lived lives that are very different from ours. We still are trying to solve deep mysteries about their civilizations.

A TRIP BACK IN TIME

Get ready to visit some of the wonders of ancient North America. In this book, *ancient* just means "old," before A.D. 1700. We will visit ancient Cahokia in Illinois. It was a thriving city with almost twenty thousand people by 1150.

Many people say that Italian explorer Christopher Columbus was the first European to set foot in North America in 1492. However, the ruins of ancient buildings discovered at Jellyfish Cove in Newfoundland, Canada, proved that theory wrong.

One wonder in this book is not an ancient city, a huge pyramid, or a magnificent monument. It is an idea that united five nations, or tribes, of Native Americans in the Iroquois Confederacy. Get ready for more interesting ideas as you turn the pages of this book.

1 Jellyfish Cove

This modern photograph, taken from above, shows the reconstructed Viking settlement at Jellyfish Cove, Newfoundland, Canada.

ANCIENT ADVENTURE STORIES, OR SAGAS, SAID THAT LEIF ERIKSSON SAILED SHIPS FROM EUROPE TO VINLAND ABOUT A.D. 1000. ERIKSSON WAS A FAMOUS LEADER OF THE VIKINGS. THESE SEAGOING PEOPLE LIVED IN THE PRESENT-DAY SCANDINAVIAN COUNTRIES OF NORWAY, DENMARK, AND SWEDEN. THE SAGAS DESCRIBED HOW THE VIKINGS BUILT HOUSES AND LIVED IN VINLAND. FROM DESCRIPTIONS IN THE STORIES, VINLAND SEEMED TO BE IN NORTH AMERICA. IF THOSE STORIES WERE TRUE, THE VIKINGS HAD LANDED IN THE NEW WORLD ALMOST FIVE HUNDRED YEARS BEFORE CHRISTOPHER COLUMBUS'S VOYAGE IN 1492.

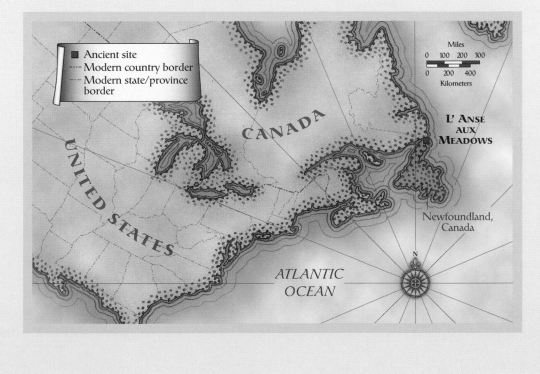

This nineteenth-century painting shows Viking Leif Eriksson and his shipmates landing in North America. The painting is at the Library of Congress in Washington, D.C.

Modern archaeologists, however, could not find any proof. Archaeologists study ancient times and peoples by examining what is left of their artifacts—belongings such as buildings, tools, dishes, and weapons. After years of searching for the ruins of Eriksson's Vinland settlement, archaeologists began to think that the stories were not true. After all, they were not written down until three hundred years after the events they described. Storytellers in ancient Scandinavia had memorized the stories. When passed down from one generation to another, people may have gotten them wrong.

But in 1960, a Norwegian explorer named Helge Ingstad finally found evidence that Vinland did exist. Following an ancient map, he found mysterious, grassy mounds. Ingstad found the mounds near L'Anse aux Meadows, which means Jellyfish Cove. French fishermen who settled this area gave it its name. The village is on the island of Newfoundland in eastern Canada.

DIGGING UP THE TRUTH

In 1961 Ingstad returned to Jellyfish Cove with his wife, Anne Stine. She was an archaeologist. Stine dug into the mounds and soon discovered a hole lined with flat rocks. It was a cooking pit, just like those used by the Vikings in ancient Norway. Stine immediately suspected that Vikings had lived in this settlement.

In 1963 Norwegian explorer Helge Ingstad pointed on a map to the location of Jellyfish Cove, where he found a Viking settlement.

Over the next eight years, Stine and her team of archaeologists excavated more artifacts. They were similar to those found in Viking settlements in Scandinavia. The archaeologists unearthed the foundations of eight buildings. In one building, they found the kind of bronze ring that Vikings had used to fasten their cloaks. Another building had a carved stone oil lamp that Vikings had used to light their sod (grass-covered) houses.

The archaeologists found a bone needle used for knitting, iron nails identical to those used in Viking ships, and other Viking artifacts. Carbon-14 tests on charred wood showed that Vikings were at Jellyfish Cove in about A.D. 1000. Artifacts at Jellyfish Cove proved that Christopher Columbus was not the first European to land in North America.

DRAGON SHIPS

Many people think of Vikings as fierce people who wore horned helmets and were interested only in fighting and attacking villages along the coasts of northern Europe. The word *Viking* does mean "pirate." The Vikings did get a bad reputation by attacking and robbing people in England, Ireland, and Scotland. But they also set up trading centers.

Jellyfish Cove

This twentieth-century painting by U.S. artist N. C. Wyeth shows Vikings in their ships crossing the Atlantic Ocean.

All Vikings weren't traders. Many had settled lives in Norway, Sweden, and Denmark. Most Vikings were farmers or fishers. Vikings were great artists and craftspeople. They made beautiful objects from gold, silver, stone, iron, and wood. Vikings sailed to other parts of Europe and peacefully traded goods with other people.

The Vikings invented a new kind of ship, the longboat or longship. They used it for raids, trading, and exploration. Longships were equipped with both oars and a brightly colored sail. They were fast and strong and could sail through rough ocean waters. Some were almost 70 feet (23 meters) long and 16 feet (5 m) wide. The Vikings' enemies sometimes called these boats dragon ships, because they had dragonlike carvings on the front.

Vikings sailed those ships along the

BURIED *in a Boat*

The Vikings sometimes buried kings and warriors in their boats. They placed the body in the boat, along with gold, weapons, and other valuable possessions. People then buried the whole boat. Archaeologists have discovered several of these ship burials.

> *"They had a fast ship with twelve or thirteen oars on each side and a crew of about thirteen men. The ship was richly painted above the sea line and magnificently decorated . . . and it had a blue and red striped sail. . . . It was fully rigged with tents and provisions."*
>
> —from Egil's Saga, *an ancient Viking story believed to be written by Snorri Sturluson between A.D. 1220 and 1240*

coast of Scandinavia and into the open ocean in search of new lands. After building settlements on Greenland, they sailed farther west.

VIKINGS VISIT VINLAND

Sometime around 1000, Eriksson landed at Jellyfish Cove. Although Newfoundland is chilly, it seemed pleasant to people from the cold lands of Scandinavia and Greenland. According to the sagas, Eriksson "gave the land a name in accordance with the good things they [the Vikings] found in it, calling it Vinland." The Vikings found lush green meadows of grass and trees. Rivers were brimming with salmon and other fish, and there were plenty of other wild animals for food.

Leif Eriksson and his crew built houses made of sod and probably wood or stone at Jellyfish Cove. The settlement became a base camp. The crew used it to explore the surrounding area. Ancient sagas say that groups of Vikings made four additional voyages to Jellyfish Cove, staying in Eriksson's houses. One voyage may have brought 135 men and 15 women to the settlement.

The Vikings probably used the settlement for only a few years. We do not know why the Vikings left, rather than establishing a permanent settlement. Archaeologists think that Native American people may have chased them away.

Another idea is that the Vikings did not get along with one another. They may have fought among themselves, hurting or killing many people. With such violence, perhaps nobody wanted to live at Jellyfish Cove. The survivors may have gone home and never returned.

In the 1400s, the Vikings also left their settlements in Greenland and returned to Scandinavia. We do not know why they left. Some archaeologists think that Earth's climate turned cooler, making Greenland too cold for people to live there.

A MODERN WONDER

The ancient Viking buildings at Jellyfish Cove have been reconstructed, and this wonder of the ancient world is well protected. In 1977 the Historic Sites and Monuments Board of Canada named Jellyfish Cove a National Historic Site. To preserve this wonder for future generations, the United Nations Educational, Scientific, and Cultural Organization (UNESCO) chose Jellyfish Cove as a World Heritage Site in 1978 because of what it tells about the worldwide movement of peoples.

Exhibits in a visitor center operated by Parks Canada describe Jellyfish Cove's history and help tourists understand the Viking way of life. Some of the displays include artifacts unearthed by Helge Ingstad and Anne Stine in the 1960s. Parks Canada's staff sometimes dress up in Viking costumes. They offer tourists a feeling of what it might have been like to live in Jellyfish Cove. They give tours of the settlement. Visitors also can hike along trails to see the surrounding landscape. It looks much the same as it did more than one thousand years ago, when Leif Eriksson landed.

Know Your F, U, THs?

The Vikings' written language used symbols called runes. The rune alphabet began with symbols for *F, U,* and *TH,* just as our modern alphabet starts with *A, B,* and *C.* Runes were used as symbols, especially to protect warriors on the battlefield. Vikings also carved runes into large stones *(below).* The stones were set upright in the ground and used as grave markers or to tell stories.

Top: *Visitors walk around the reconstructed Viking settlement at Jellyfish Cove.* Left: *A fire lights the inside of a longhouse at the reconstructed settlement.*

2 THE *Iroquois* CONFEDERACY

Iroquois leader Hiawatha is shown in this painting. He was instrumental in convincing Native American tribes to live in peace.

*T*HE LEADERS OF THE THIRTEEN AMERICAN COLONIES DECLARED INDEPENDENCE FROM BRITISH RULE ON JULY 4, 1776. BUT THEY STARTED GATHERING IDEAS FOR A NEW GOVERNMENT EVEN EARLIER. AS THE COLONISTS PREPARED TO DRAFT THE U.S. CONSTITUTION, THEY BORROWED SOME IDEAS FROM GREAT THINKERS IN EUROPE. THEY ALSO USED SOME IDEAS ABOUT DEMOCRACY FROM PATRIOTS AND WRITERS IN THE COLONIES.

Some historians think that Benjamin Franklin, John Rutledge, and other colonial leaders also took ideas for the Constitution from yet another source—from the Iroquois Confederacy. Many Native American tribes, or nations, often fought against one another. But one amazing group of nations decided to form a confederacy. They agreed to live together peacefully and govern themselves under a constitution. And they lived that way for hundreds of years.

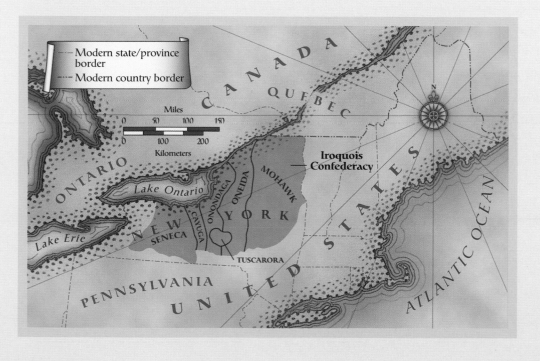

The Iroquois Confederacy, which still exists, is believed to be the oldest continuing "participatory democracy" in the world. In such a government, all members of a community participate and have a vote on major decisions. When Europeans first arrived in North America, the Iroquois Confederacy ruled a huge area of the northeastern United States and southern Canada. The confederacy included parts of modern-day Ontario and Quebec in Canada, the modern-day U.S. states of Pennsylvania and New York, and parts of the New England region of the United States.

The Iroquois Confederacy originally included five nations. They were the Mohawk, the Oneida, the Onondaga, the Cayuga, and the Seneca. Members called their confederacy Kanonsionni, which means the "way of the longhouse." (A longhouse was a large building made from the framework of tree branches and covered with sheets of tree bark.) They thought of themselves as nations living together peacefully as a family in the same longhouse. The Mohawk guarded the imaginary door on the east. The Seneca guarded the imaginary door on the western end. The Onondaga village, in the middle, was the capital, or meeting place, of the confederacy's council. A sixth nation, the Tuscarora, joined the confederacy later. Then it changed its name to the Haudenosaunee, or "people of the longhouse."

This symbol of the Iroquois Confederacy is a woodcut from the 1600s. The five original tribes that belonged to the confederacy are represented by animals at the corners and one tribe as the symbol for the village in the middle.

"Their hearts shall be full of peace and good will and their minds filled with a yearning for the welfare of the people of the Confederacy. With endless patience they shall carry out their duty and their firmness shall be tempered with a tenderness for their people."

— *constitution of the Iroquois nations, describing members of the Great Council, ca. A.D. 1390–1500*

VILLAGES OF LONGHOUSES

In fact, the Iroquois did live in longhouses. Some of these buildings were 100 feet (31 m) long. An entire clan, or family group, of about sixty people might live in the same longhouse. The Iroquois people lived in villages. Iroquois men were in charge of hunting, trading, and war. They fished in rivers and hunted for deer, rabbits, and other wild animals. Women did most of the farming. They grew corn, beans, and squash, and they picked wild berries.

Below: *This nineteenth-century illustration shows an Iroquois longhouse and Iroquois people going about daily chores. A longhouse is also shown being constructed in the background.* Right: *The interior of this longhouse has been reconstructed at Ganondagon State Historic Site in Ontario County, New York. It was the site of a Seneca village and was known as the western gateway to the Iroquois Confederacy.*

Clans were descended from the women's families. Iroquois women ruled the clans. They made decisions about farming, property, and other matters. Each clan had a clan mother, an important position. Clan mothers chose the representatives to the Great Council. These representatives governed the Iroquois Confederacy. Although women elected members of the Great Council, only men could serve on the council.

Hiawatha is shown fishing in this illustration from The Poetical Works of Henry Wadsworth Longfellow, *published in 1879.*

DREAMS OF
the Iroquois

The Iroquois believed that dreams could come true. They relied on dreams as clues for making the right choices in life. Dreams helped the Iroquois decide whom to marry. Dreams also helped them decide when to hunt and where to fish (below). If one member of a hunting party dreamed of failure, the whole group would turn around and go back home. The Iroquois even had a dream-sharing ritual. Groups of people got together and shared their dreams. In that way, people got opinions on what a dream meant and how to use it as a guide in life.

"The proceedings of the Great Council . . . were anciently formal, always commencing [starting] with an expression of Gratitude to the Great Spirit for bringing all safely on their journeys to the place of meeting."

—E. M. Chadwick, describing the Iroquois government in 1897

THE GREAT COUNCIL

Legends say that before the confederacy was formed, the original five tribes constantly argued and fought with one another. Finally, two great prophets—religious leaders Ayonwentah (Hiawatha) and Dekanawidah (the Peacemaker)—convinced the tribes to live in peace. Once the nations stopped fighting, they agreed to live under a constitution. This set of rules was known as the Great Law of Peace. That constitution provided for a democratic form of government. In a democracy, a majority of the people—rather than a king—make important decisions.

The Iroquois people left no written records. So we do not know exactly when the constitution was established. Recent studies seem to indicate that it was formed as early as the mid-1100s.

Each Iroquois nation sent representatives to serve on the Great Council. By the height of its power in the 1600s, the confederacy had about twelve thousand people. Although members spoke different languages, the languages were of the same Iroquoian family.

During council meetings, leaders discussed and debated political matters. Then they voted. Afterward, each Great Council member took those decisions back to his own nation. Each Iroquois nation also had its own tribal council,

EVER *Wonder?*

How did the Iroquois remember their constitution without a written language? Tribes selected people to memorize the Great Law of Peace. The words then were passed down from older people to younger people and generation to generation. To help them remember, the Iroquois used wampum. These belts of colored beads were woven into patterns that had special meanings and expressed the ideas in the Great Law of Peace.

This 1940 painting by American artist Howard Chandler Christy shows the signing of the U.S. Constitution in 1787 in Philadelphia. It is on display in the Capitol Building in Washington, D.C.

which followed the Great Council's rulings. But each tribal council made its own rules and decisions about local matters.

MODEL FOR U.S. CONSTITUTION?

The government of the Iroquois is similar to the system of government the U.S. Constitution established. The Constitution, for instance, allows states to have their own governments. But state laws must follow the laws of the U.S. federal government. Historians disagree about just how much influence the Iroquois had on the founders of the United States.

We do know that Benjamin Franklin and other colonial leaders knew about the Great Law of Peace. They attended meetings of the Great Council and saw Iroquois government in action. Some historians say Benjamin Franklin used Iroquois ideas in an early plan for a colonial government that he wrote in 1754.

John Rutledge, a delegate to the Constitutional Convention of 1787 (at which the U.S. Constitution was written), mentioned the Iroquois Great Law of Peace several times. He even quoted an Iroquois chief in words that sound a lot like the first lines of the U.S. Constitution. The Great Law starts "We, the people, to form a union, to establish peace, equity and order. . . . " The U.S. Constitution begins, "We the people of the United States, in order to form a more perfect union. . . . "

The American Revolution (1775–1783) divided the Iroquois Confederacy. Many Tuscarora and Oneida people fought with the colonists. Many Mohawk, Seneca, Onondaga, and Cayuga people fought with the British against the colonists. After the war, many Iroquois loyal to Britain moved to Canada.

Members of the Onondaga tribe and British soldiers gather around a council fire in the 1700s in this illustration from an 1878 edition of the magazine Scribner's Monthly.

> *"It would be a very strange thing if [the] Six Nations . . . should be capable of forming a [constitution] for such an Union and be able to execute it in such a manner . . . and yet a like Union should be impracticable for ten or a dozen English colonies."*
> —Benjamin Franklin, writing about the Iroquois Confederacy's constitution in 1751

There, the British gave them free land as a reward. Many of those loyal to the colonists stayed in their original regions on reservations, land the U.S. government set aside for Native Americans.

A MODERN WONDER

The Iroquois Great Council continues to meet. It still follows some rules of the Great Law of Peace. Modern-day governments of the individual Iroquois nations, however, make most of the decisions once left to the Great Council.

Iroquois people no longer live in longhouses. Instead, they live in modern homes and apartments. Some live in towns and cities. Others live together in settlements and on

AN IROQUOIS GIFT TO MODERN SPORTS: *Lacrosse*

The Iroquois people invented lacrosse *(shown below)*, a popular modern team sport. Using sticks with nets on the end, lacrosse players try to score goals by putting the ball into the other team's goal. French explorers named the game lacrosse. Instead of having six to twelve players—as they do in the modern game—Iroquois teams had one hundred to one thousand players. Their playing fields could be more than 1 mile (1.6 kilometer) long. Matches lasted from sunrise to sunset, for two or three days. Ancient lacrosse was not a game. Instead, tribes used it to settle arguments and to train young men for war.

reservations in Canada, New York State, Oklahoma, and Wisconsin. Reservations welcome tourists and other visitors.

This hut (below) *made of bark and these log canoes* (left) *are part of a reconstructed Iroquois fishing camp on the Susquehanna River in New York.*

3 Cahokia

This aerial photograph shows the mounds at Cahokia Mounds State Historic Site in Illinois. The mounds are part of the ruins of the ancient Native American city of Cahokia.

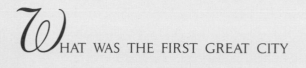HAT WAS THE FIRST GREAT CITY IN THE LAND THAT BECAME THE UNITED STATES? MANY PEOPLE WOULD PROBABLY NAME A COLONIAL CITY SUCH AS PHILADELPHIA, BOSTON, OR NEW YORK. THOSE WERE LARGE CITIES BEFORE THE AMERICAN COLONIES BECAME INDEPENDENT IN 1776. BUT ANOTHER BIG CITY EXISTED HUNDREDS OF YEARS EARLIER.

That first large city in what later became the United States was Cahokia. Cahokia is in Illinois, across the Mississippi River from the city of Saint Louis, Missouri. Cahokia's population had reached about twenty thousand people by A.D. 1150, making it larger than most European cities at that time. Not until the late 1700s did Philadelphia finally get more people than Cahokia. We don't know the original name of the city. Cahokia got its name from a group of Native Americans who lived near the location in the 1600s.

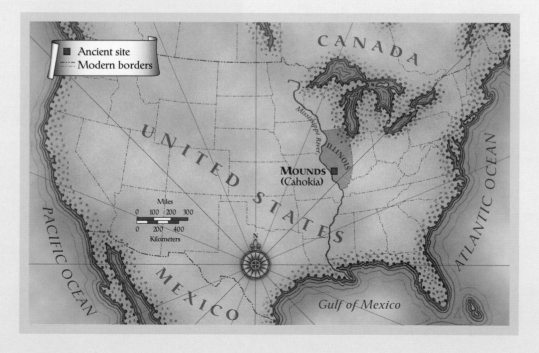

Cahokia was the center of a great, ancient North American culture that archaeologists call Mississippian. This culture arose in the Mississippi River valley in the modern-day state of Illinois. Its origin is unknown. This culture developed there because soil in the Mississippi River valley was so rich. In those days, people plowed by hand. Soil near Cahokia was soft and easy to plow compared to the hard soil of the surrounding area.

Farmers surrounding the city could grow enough food to sustain twenty thousand people year-round. The Mississippian culture developed and thrived because the people no longer had to be hunters and gatherers. Instead of roaming from place to place, they could stay put. They settled into villages. They became artisans and tradespeople and developed an orderly society. An elite

Community life in Cahokia is shown in this drawing. On the left, tribe members build one of the houses in the village.

EVER *Wonder?*

Why did the ancient Mississippian people build their capitol at Cahokia?

Cahokia was an almost perfect place for a city. It had rich soil for growing crops, and the Mississippi River provided water for drinking and fish to eat. Deer lived in forests to the southwest of Cahokia. They provided food and skins for rawhide clothing. The forests also provided trees for firewood and buildings. Wooded areas to the east had nuts, berries, and more wild animals for food. Prairie with tall grass for making mats and the thatched roofs of houses lay to the north. And a hard rock called chert could be used for stone tools and weapons.

Above: *This modern photograph of Monk's Mound shows the staircase visitors can climb that leads to the top of the mound.* Left: *Monk's Mound is shown in the mid-nineteenth century in this drawing.*

class governed a lower class, such as workers, farmers, and potters.

The people living in the area built mounds of earth. They built as many as 120 mounds. Some of these mounds were gigantic.

MAKING MONK'S MOUND

Monk's Mound was the largest prehistoric earthen structure in North America. The mound got its name from a group of French monks (members of a religious order) who began farming the mound in the 1800s. By that time, Cahokia had been abandoned for hundreds of years.

When Monk's Mound was built, ancient workers had no earthmovers or other modern machinery. Each worker carried a basket of earth that probably

This 1990 painting by William R. Iseminger shows an aerial view of Cahokia, with Monk's Mound and the Grand Plaza in the center.

weighed about 60 pounds (27 kilograms). That is almost as much as seven 1-gallon (3.8-liter) jugs of milk.

Each worker dumped one basket of earth on the mound and then climbed down to refill the basket. The worker filled another basket, carried it to the building site, and dumped that soil onto the pile. Monk's Mound covered an area the size of fourteen football fields placed side by side. Workers made a mound of earth 100 feet

THE BIRDMAN *Tablet*

While excavating Monk's Mound, archaeologists discovered the Birdman Tablet. The tablet is a flat piece of sandstone carved with mysterious images. On the front was a person dressed in a mask and eagle's feathers. Carved on the back was a pattern that looked like a snake's skin. Archaeologists do not yet know the purpose of the Birdman Tablet.

(30 m) high, about the height of a ten-story building. The project took about two hundred years to finish.

At the top of Monk's Mound was a large wooden building—about 100 feet (30 m) long, 48 feet (15 m) wide, and 50 feet (15 m) high. Archaeologists think it was a religious temple or a palace for Cahokia's ruler.

Monk's Mound was in the center of Cahokia. About one hundred smaller mounds were built throughout the city. Rulers and other civic leaders built large homes on top of the mounds. They could actually look down on others. A 2-mile-long (3 km) wall surrounded the center of the city. Archaeologists think that the wall was built to defend Cahokia from enemies.

MARVELOUS MISSISSIPPIANS

Native American tribes probably began adopting a settled way of life around A.D. 800. The city had homes for common people, workshops to make tools and pottery, markets, and open plazas. The Grand Plaza, for instance, was the size of fifty football fields. People gathered in the plazas for ceremonies, celebrations, parades, and sports. One popular sports event was *chunkey*. Two players holding poles or swords ran as another rolled a stone ring. Both players threw spears or poles toward the ring. They tried to land the poles as close as

This painting shows the view across the Grand Plaza to Monk's Mound in Cahokia. Villagers are playing chunkey *in the plaza. This mural was painted by Lloyd K. Townsend in 1989.*

This transparency by Michael Hampshire from 1989 shows Cahokian people bargaining for goods in the marketplace. Monk's Mound looms in the background on the right.

possible to where they thought the ring would fall over. Spectators often placed bets on the outcome.

In addition to building mounds, the Native Americans farmed the fields around Cahokia. They grew corn, squash, pumpkins, and beans. The potters of Cahokia put designs on their pottery that reflected the farm products.

The Cahokian people made arrow-points and stone tools. Craftspeople made necklaces from stone, copper, and other materials gathered from nearby streams.

Most Cahokian people lived in homes built from a framework of tree branches covered with mats made from reeds, cattail plants, or grass. Some larger buildings got a coating of daub, a plasterlike paste of wet clay mixed with chopped-up grass. When the coating dried, it became hard. The daub coating strengthened the building and made it waterproof.

Unfortunately, the Cahokia people left no written records of their culture.

MOUND OF THE *Ruler-Priest*

Inside one mound at Cahokia, archaeologists found a skeleton of a man in his early forties. He had been buried about 1050. The archaeologists named it the Mound of the Ruler-Priest. The skeleton may have been the remains of an important ruler of Cahokia. The man's body lay on a bed of twenty thousand shell ornaments and more than eight hundred arrows. Almost sixty other people had been sacrificed, or killed, and buried with the man. Fifty-three of them were young women. Four men had had their heads and hands cut off. The human sacrifices may have been part of a ceremony to honor the ruler.

Cahokian people gather crops of maize and squash in this illustration. It is from an 1890 book on early inhabitants of North America.

Archaeologists get information about Cahokia from artifacts and clues left behind in the city's ruins. The wall, for instance, is a clue that the Cahokia people had enemies. Parts of the wall were not built as evenly and neatly as others. Archaeologists think those parts were built in a hurry, perhaps because an enemy was about to attack.

Some necklaces left behind by the Cahokians are made with shell beads. Some of the shells used are found only along the coast of the Atlantic Ocean. Others are found only along the Gulf of Mexico coast. These hint that this culture traded with people living far away. Cahokia may have been so famous and wealthy that people came from hundreds of miles away to trade and visit.

STONEHENGE?
No, Woodhenge

Stonehenge is an ancient stone monument in southwestern England. It is made up of a circle of huge, upright stone pillars supporting flat stone slabs. The Cahokian people built a ring of wooden posts *(below)*. When they are aligned with an outer post, they work as calendars. The wooden posts lined up with the rising sun at certain times of the year. In doing so, they marked important times of the year, such as the start of summer and winter. Archaeologists called this formation Woodhenge. The Cahokians built several woodhenges over the centuries. Workers at the state park have reconstructed a model of Woodhenge.

MYSTERIOUS MOUNDS

By about 1100, Cahokia had become the center of the Mississippian culture. For unknown reasons, the Cahokian culture began to decline about 1200. By 1400 Cahokia was a ghost town. As years passed, its wood-and-mud buildings fell apart, and everyone forgot that Cahokia existed. The city's real name also was forgotten. The name "Cahokia" came from the Cahokia Indians who lived nearby in the late 1600s.

> *"[T]he Indians were the authors of all the ancient monuments of the Mississippi Valley and Gulf States. . . . The historical evidence is, as we have seen, conclusive that some of the tribes of Indians were mound builders."*
> —Cyrus Thomas, U.S. archaeologist, 1894

The mounds did remain, however. They created a great mystery as pioneers moved westward and saw these amazing structures. People refused to believe that Native Americans could have built the mounds. They said the mounds were built by Vikings or other Europeans who came to America and disappeared.

In the 1890s, a U.S. archaeologist named Cyrus Thomas studied artifacts from the mounds. Thomas realized that Native Americans had built the mounds. He wrote a report that helped other people to understand these wonders of ancient North America.

A MODERN WONDER

The remains of Cahokia are preserved in the Cahokia Mounds State Historic Site. The site is located near the city of Saint Louis, Missouri. Cahokia is also a UNESCO World Heritage Site. Visitors can climb a modern stairway to the top of Monk's Mound. From the top, they get an excellent view of Cahokia's ruins, the city of Saint Louis, and the Mississippi River.

Mounds and other remains of the Mississippian culture, however, are not well protected. Construction of farms, highways, and cities has damaged or destroyed many mounds and artifacts.

4 Cliff Palace

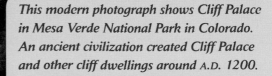

This modern photograph shows Cliff Palace in Mesa Verde National Park in Colorado. An ancient civilization created Cliff Palace and other cliff dwellings around A.D. 1200.

$\mathcal{I}$N DECEMBER OF 1888, TWO
COWBOYS, RICHARD WETHERILL AND CHARLIE MASON, RODE
THEIR HORSES ACROSS MESA VERDE IN SOUTHWESTERN COLORADO.
THE COWBOYS WERE LOOKING FOR COWS THAT HAD STRAYED FROM
THE HERD.

Wetherill and Mason stopped at the edge of the mesa. *Mesa* is the Spanish word for "table," and *verde* means "green." (A mesa is a broad, flat hilltop.) They gazed across a deep canyon. The cowboys expected to see bare rock and soil on the tall, steep cliffs across the way. Instead, what looked like a "magnificent city" was nestled on the ledge of one cliff. The cowboys had seen small cliff houses, or dwellings, before. However, this dwelling was so big and beautiful that it seemed to be a palace where some ancient king had once lived.

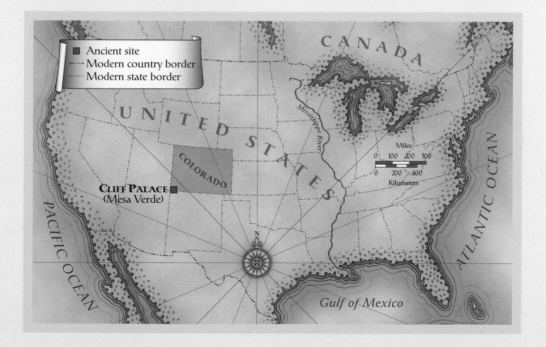

This photograph from around 1900 shows the Cliff Palace ruins. A man sits on top of the round structure in the center of the image.

They called the site Cliff Palace. Wetherill and Mason may have been the first white men to see the famous cliff dwellings at Mesa Verde. Cliff Palace was among hundreds of cliff dwellings that had been occupied by the people of an ancient civilization.

These people are sometimes called the "Anasazi," a Navajo Indian word meaning "ancient ones." They were ancestors of many tribes of Native Americans in the southwestern United States. The Anasazi lived in the Four Corners area, where the modern states of New Mexico, Utah, Colorado, and Arizona meet.

LIFE ON THE GREEN TABLE

Sometime in the A.D. 500s, the Anasazi moved onto Mesa Verde. At first, the Anasazi lived in pit houses. They dug circular holes in the ground. Then they covered the top with a roof made from sticks held together with dried mud. About 1100 the

SPANISH *Influence*

Spanish explorers who later traveled through the Four Corners area called the villages they saw "pueblos," the Spanish word for "town." As a result, the Native Americans in the region became known as Pueblo Indians. Spanish explorers also picked the name Mesa Verde. The name was perfect for the high plateau covered with small pine trees and bushes. Spanish explorers, however, apparently never saw the cliff dwellings.

"From the rim of the canyon we had our first view of Cliff Palace. . . . To me this is the grandest view of all among the ancient ruins of the Southwest. We spent several hours going from room to room, and picked up several articles . . . among them a stone axe with the handle still on it. There were several parts of human skeletons scattered about."

—Charlie Mason, 1888

Anasazi started building remarkable stone structures aboveground. These structures were ancient apartment buildings. They had several stories, and hundreds of rooms—enough to hold a whole village of people.

While living on the mesa, the Anasazi hunted deer, bison, and other animals. The Anasazi also grew corn, beans, and squash. They must have been excellent farmers because the soil in the area is very dry most of the year. Archaeologists have found the ruins of dams and irrigation systems that these ancient people built. (Dams control the flow of water. Farmers use irrigation systems to water crops.) Archaeologists also know that the Anasazi wove and decorated baskets and made beautiful pottery. Archaeologists have found those artifacts in the ruins of Anasazi settlements.

Archaeologists think that the Anasazi probably used the cliffs while living on Mesa Verde. The cliffs had many flat ledges and cavelike areas. Children probably climbed down to the ledges to play. Adults could have stored food

These artifacts were found in the ruins at Mesa Verde around 1900. The artifacts include pieces of fabric, pottery fragments, a bowl, and a pitcher.

on the cliffs or slept there during good weather. However, the Anasazi did not build Cliff Palace and other dwellings until about 1200.

CLINGING TO THE CLIFFS

We do not know why most of the Anasazi moved from the mesa onto the cliffs. Perhaps they moved to the cliffs for protection against enemies. There must have been important reasons. The cavelike cliff dwellings would have been damp and dark compared to houses on the mesa. Cliff dwellers were also further away from sources of water and food. In addition, it took a huge effort to build the cliff dwellings.

The Anasazi built hundreds of houses on the cliffs. Many were small, with one or two rooms. Some were just a cave with a wall and door built at the opening. Others, however, had many rooms. Some were similar to modern apartment or office buildings, with rooms on different levels. Those included the dwellings later named Cliff Palace, Long House, Spruce Tree House, and Balcony House.

This 1878 illustration from Scribner's Monthly shows the Anasazi in their cliff dwellings under attack from enemies.

"What can have induced a people to have recourse to dwelling places [so difficult to reach]? The answer must be that nothing short of the ever imminent attacks of a hostile people can have driven the cliff dwellers to these . . . mountain fortresses, which afforded a safe refuge, so long as food and water held out."

—Gustaf Nordenskiold, a Swedish archaeologist who studied the cliff dwellings in the 1890s

ANCIENT Rock Climbers

Some cliff dwellings are built into the sides of steep cliffs that seem impossible to reach. How did the Anasazi people get to and from those houses? They probably used hand and toe holds in the rock— almost like modern rock climbers. Inside their houses, the Anasazi used ladders rather than stairways to go upstairs and downstairs.

Above: *This modern photo shows the Spruce Tree House in Mesa Verde National Park.*
Below: *Balcony House is another ancient cliff dwelling found in the park.*

Larger dwellings were made from blocks of sandstone, a soft stone that can be cut and shaped easily with tools made of harder rock. Stone chisels, for instance, were used to cut and smooth the blocks. Workers pounded the chisels with stone hammers. The blocks were used to build walls. The builders stuck them together with mortar made from soil, ashes, and water. Tree trunks served as beams to support floors and roofs.

Ancient people in other parts of the United States and Mexico lived in cliff dwellings. Cliff Palace, however, was the largest cliff dwelling in North America. It had 150 rooms, with perhaps one hundred people living inside. The Anasazi may have used Cliff Palace as a government center, where rulers or other important people lived, or for religious ceremonies. The palace had more than twenty circular rooms called kivas. They were used for ceremonies and social gatherings. Cliff House also had a large towerlike structure, which may have had a special but unknown purpose.

Studying Cliff House and other dwellings has helped archaeologists learn about how the Anasazi lived. In kivas, for instance, they have found the remains of Anasazi food. These ancient people cooked meals of corn, wild parsley, wild carrot, and a grain called amaranth. The Anasazi also ate meat. We know that because archaeologists found the burnt bones of turkey, rabbits, and deer left in campfire ashes. Bits of charcoal tell us that Anasazi cooks burned sagebrush and pine for fuel.

GHOST PALACE

After all the work that went into building these amazing structures, the Anasazi lived in the cliff dwellings for only seventy-five to one hundred years. Between 1250 and 1300, the Anasazi abandoned their homes on the cliffs and moved south. The cliff dwellings became a ghost town.

We do not know why the Anasazi people left Mesa Verde.

Anasazi women grind corn in this illustration from an 1890 book on the early people who lived in North America.

> "[This] country once supported a great population, a people well advanced in many arts, and who conceived of certain forms of beauty. . . . And may we not imagine them as a race who loved peace rather than war?"
> —Frederick Chapin, who wrote a book about the cliff dwellers in 1892

Above: *The view from above Cliff Palace shows the kivas in front of the stone structures. The towerlike structure can be seen on the right side of the image. Researchers aren't sure what the Anasazi people used the tower for. Left: This close-up view of a kiva shows the stones that make up the walls of the ceremonial rooms.*

Some scientists believe they were driven away by a great drought that struck the Four Corners region in 1275. This area normally got very little rain. Even less rain fell for the next twenty-five years. Without water to drink and to grow crops, life at Mesa Verde may have become impossible.

The Anasazi culture did not completely disappear, however. Other Native Americans living in the Four Corners region imitated the Anasazi. For example, archaeologists think that the Mogollon people learned how to build stone houses from the Anasazi. The Mogollons lived in modern-day Arizona and New Mexico. Native Americans in other areas copied Anasazi ways of making and decorating pottery.

Richard Wetherill and Charlie Mason, of course, told their friends and families about the cliff dwellings. They explored the ruins, and other people did the same. In those days, it was acceptable for visitors to take home pottery, baskets, tools, necklaces, and other artifacts. Visitors camped in the cliff dwellings, knocked down walls, and caused other damage to the ruins as they explored and looked for artifacts.

SPOOKY *Wonder*

Native Americans of the Navajo and Ute tribes moved into the Four Corners area about two hundred years after the Anasazi left. However, they stayed away from the Cliff Palace and other ancient dwellings. They believed that spirits of the ancient ones still lived at Mesa Verde.

This image from the early 1920s shows visitors to Cliff Palace standing among the cliff dwellings. In the early 1900s, tourists caused damage to the ruins as they explored.

Ever Wonder?

How do we know that a drought happened just before the Anasazi left Mesa Verde?

Scientists discovered that information from studying tree rings in logs. A tree adds one ring to its trunk every year. In years with plenty of rain, the tree grows more and the rings are thicker. By counting and measuring the rings, scientists can see a record of weather over a long period of time. Logs from the Four Corners area had unusually thin rings for almost twenty-five years, from about 1275 to 1300. The Anasazi left Mesa Verde during this time.

A Modern Wonder

In 1906 U.S. president Theodore Roosevelt decided to protect the cliff dwellings from further damage. He established Mesa Verde National Park to preserve the remains of the ancient Anasazi civilization. Three years later, in 1909, Jesse Walter Fewkes of the Smithsonian Institution excavated and stabilized Cliff Palace.

Modern-day Mesa Verde National Park includes six hundred cliff dwellings and thousands of other archaeological sites with remains of the Anasazi people. To protect the dwellings, visitors are no longer allowed to walk through the dwellings alone. Instead, park rangers escort visitors on tours of Cliff Palace and other dwellings.

Cliff Palace at Mesa Verde National Park attracts many visitors every year.

The rain forest surrounds the remains of the ancient Mayan city of Palenque, built around A.D. 615 in present-day southern Mexico.

$\mathcal{T}$HE MAYA WERE AN ANCIENT NATIVE AMERICAN PEOPLE. THEY DEVELOPED A MAGNIFICENT CIVILIZATION IN SOUTHERN MEXICO AND PARTS OF CENTRAL AMERICA. THE TEMPLE OF THE INSCRIPTIONS AND PAKAL'S PALACE ARE IN THE ANCIENT MAYA CITY OF PALENQUE IN SOUTHERN MEXICO. WE KNOW VERY LITTLE ABOUT THE CITY'S HISTORY—NOT EVEN ITS ANCIENT NAME. THE MODERN NAME CAME FROM THE NEARBY SPANISH VILLAGE OF SANTO DOMINGO DE PALENQUE.

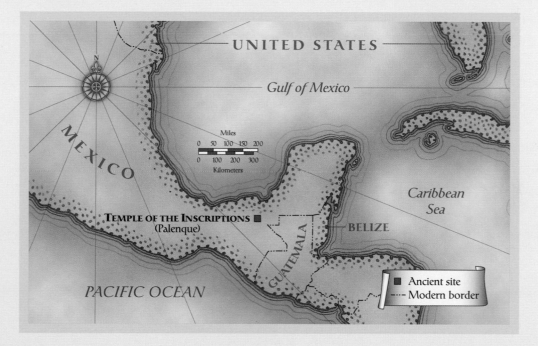

People probably began living in the area about 300 B.C. For hundreds of years, Palenque was probably a small farming village. Many kings and queens had ruled over the years. Pakal came to power in A.D. 615, at the age of twelve. He started building Palenque into a great city. Pakal ruled for almost seventy years. Such stability undoubtedly contributed to creating Palenque's golden age (between 600 and 750).

More than a thousand years later, the work of Mexican archaeologist Alberto Ruz Lhuillier shed light on the city and its greatest ruler. In 1949 Ruz noticed something strange inside the Temple of the Inscriptions. This temple-pyramid towers 75 feet (23 m) above Palenque. Maya workers built the temple-pyramid from stone blocks. The largest blocks weighed almost 15 tons (14 metric tons). Those blocks were stacked to form a pyramid 84 feet (25 m) long and both 38 feet (12 m) wide and high. A long, wide stone staircase leads to the temple's entrance.

The temple was named for the hieroglyphic-like inscriptions carved on its stone walls. Maya writing is a system that uses symbols to represent ideas and sounds. The inscriptions in this temple are among the longest in Maya culture.

OH BOY, *What a King!*

Pakal became king of Palenque in 615 when he was just twelve years old. Adults in the royal family probably helped Pakal make decisions until he got older and learned how to rule. Boy oh boy, did Pakal ever learn well. He ruled Palenque for almost seventy years until his death in 683.

Alberto Ruz Lhuillier inside the Temple of the Inscriptions. His team worked for years inside the ruins.

Ruz and his team found this hidden stairway in the Temple of the Inscriptions. They worked for four years to discover where it led.

But Ruz wasn't looking at the inscriptions. He was looking at the floor. Someone had drilled holes into one of the slabs in the stone floor. Ruz had been studying the temple for years, but he had never noticed the holes before. They made him suspect that the stone slab covered a secret chamber hidden below the floor. Maybe ancient Maya workers had drilled holes to string rope under the slab of rock. Then they used the rope to lower the slab into place.

After discovery of the secret passage, Ruz's team worked for four years. When workers lifted the slab, they discovered a steep, slippery stairway underneath. It was filled with rubble. Ruz had to remove the rubble to get down that stairway. At the bottom of the dark stairwell, 90 feet (27 m) below the floor, was a tomb. Inside, hidden for more than one thousand years, was the skeleton of Pakal the Great. Pakal was Palenque's most famous ruler.

Never before had archaeologists discovered an ancient Maya king buried

"Out of the dim shadows emerged a vision from a fairy tale, a fantastic . . . sight from another world. It seemed a huge magic [room] carved out of ice, the walls sparkling and glistening like snow crystals. . . . Then my eyes sought the floor. This was almost entirely filled with a great carved stone slab, in perfect condition."

— Alberto Ruz Lhuillier, describing his discovery of Pakal the Great's tomb in 1952

inside a pyramid. The Maya used their pyramids mainly as temples to worship their gods. Alberto Ruz Lhuillier's discovery made archaeologists realize that the Maya might have been more like the ancient Egyptians, who used pyramids as tombs for pharaohs (rulers).

Ancient Maya

The Maya took special care in burying Pakal. They placed his body in a stone sarcophagus, or coffin. Covering the coffin was a magnificently carved stone lid weighing 5 tons (4.5 metric ton). It was decorated with a fantastic carving of the Maya's World Tree. This tree connected all the Maya's ideas about life, death, and the afterlife. The carving showed Pakal as the maize god, who died and came back to life as a turtle. Carvings on the sarcophagus's sides showed Pakal's ancestors emerging from a crack in Earth.

Ruz got another surprise when he raised the lid and saw Pakal's skeleton. The Maya buried Pakal with nearly one thousand pieces of jade jewelry. This green gemstone was the ancient Maya's most precious material. A jade mask covered Pakal's face.

Pakal ordered construction of the Temple of the Inscriptions during his own lifetime. He meant it to become his own tomb. He must have ordered construction of the magnificent sarcophagus too. The door to the tomb is smaller than Pakal's sarcophagus. The tomb must have been built around the sarcophagus. When Pakal died, his son Chan Bahlum inherited the throne. He oversaw the completion of the temple and ruled for eighteen more years. The temple is Palenque's most famous building.

Some people said that Pakal got such special care because the Maya believed he was a god. Archaeologists, however, say that Pakal was honored in death because of his greatness during life. He built Palenque into a great city.

This jade burial mask lay on the face of the body in the tomb. The mask is made of individual pieces of jade, shell, and stone.

Beneath the large stone slab, Ruz and his team discovered a stone coffin. Inside was Pakal's skeleton, buried with almost a thousand pieces of jewelry.

WHO WAS BURIED IN PAKAL'S TOMB?

Archaeologists got a big surprise after they began studying Pakal the Great's skeleton. Inscriptions on the tomb said that Pakal died at the age of eighty. However, the skeleton had the teeth and bones of a person only forty years old. Younger people usually have bones that are stronger and more solid. Their teeth also are healthier, with less wear that comes from chewing hard foods.

Some archaeologists began to say that a different ruler was buried in the tomb. Most scientists now think that Pakal was buried in Pakal's tomb. They think that Pakal, being a king, ate softer food that caused less wear on his teeth. Like other people who live long, Pakal also may have been healthier and maintained a stronger body.

THE PALENQUE PALACE

Over the years, many archaeologists have worked at Palenque and helped clear away the jungle vines and dirt from the ruins. Archaeologists excavated more than thirty buildings. Almost five hundred other ancient structures may be scattered around the area, covered by thick rain forest plants and soil.

The Palenque Palace is a huge stone complex in the center of the city. The palace actually consists of several buildings. The palace probably was the home of Palenque's royal families, other nobles, priests, and important officials. Many rooms have benches that resemble thrones. Pakal renovated the palace and added rooms, vaults (rooms for keeping valuables), carved panels, patios, and courtyards. Rising above the palace is a four-story tower.

EVER *Wonder?*

How do we know that the Temple of the Inscriptions was Pakal the Great's tomb?

Archaeologists learned how to read the six hundred inscriptions on the temple walls *(below)*. That ancient writing told the history of Pakal's ancestors and his own life.

Researchers have not figured out the purpose of the tower rising above the Palenque Palace. Visitors can walk around the ruins in the rain forest in Mexico.

The tower looks like towers built in ancient European castles. No other ancient Maya city has such a tower. Some archaeologists think that Chan Bahlum's brother, Kan Xul, built the tower, but no one knows for sure, and its purpose is not known.

Palenque became a ghost town in the 900s. People abandoned it for unknown reasons. Dense jungle vines and trees soon covered Palenque, and people forgot it ever existed.

> *"We lived in the ruined palaces of their kings. Wherever we moved we saw the evidences of their [good] taste, their skills in arts, their wealth and power."*
>
> —John Lloyd Stephens, who rediscovered Palenque in 1840 and lived in the ruined city while studying it

Palenque became famous partly because it was such a surprise to Europeans when they rediscovered it in the middle of the 1800s. At the time, most people in Europe did not know that advanced civilizations existed in North America before their arrival. Two U.S. explorers, John Lloyd Stephens and Frederick Catherwood, rediscovered the ruins of Palenque in 1840. Stephens wrote a book about his discoveries and adventures that got people interested in the ancient Maya civilization.

A MODERN WONDER

To protect and preserve Palenque, the government of Mexico established a national park around the ruins in the 1930s. Palenque National Park includes 4,398 acres (1,780 hectares) of tropical rain forest. The rain forest is teeming with parrots, toucans, parrots, spider monkeys, and other wildlife. Palenque also is a UNESCO World Heritage site.

Visitors can view Palenque's Palace, the Temple of the Inscriptions, and other ruins. However, tourists may never see the fantastic treasures from Pakal's tomb. In 1985 thieves stole the jewelry and jade mask from the National Museum of Anthropology in Mexico City, where those precious objects were on display. The museum does have a replica of Pakal's tomb and many other ancient artifacts.

FIREFLY Flashlight

John Lloyd Stephens made himself right at home after rediscovering Palenque in 1840. While studying the ruins, Stephens lived in the Palenque Palace. He slept in a hammock hung in a hallway. Stevens hated the constant rain, the blood-thirsty mosquitoes, and the bats that flapped through the palace every night. However, he loved Palenque's huge fireflies. Stephens caught the insects, put them in bottles, and used their light to read at night.

Millions of tourists visit the ruins at Palenque in Mexico each year. Visitors can climb the steps to the Temple of the Inscriptions (left and below).

6 Teotihuacán

The ruins of the Pyramid of the Sun can be seen in the ancient city of Teotihuacán in central Mexico.

$\mathcal{W}$HEN PEOPLE IN MODERN MEXICO MENTION THE PYRAMIDS, THEY USUALLY DO NOT MEAN THE STONE TOMBS BUILT FOR THE PHARAOHS IN ANCIENT EGYPT. THEY MEAN PYRAMIDS AT THE ANCIENT CITY OF TEOTIHUACÁN. THE CITY IS ABOUT 30 MILES (48 KM) NORTHEAST OF MEXICO CITY. TEOTIHUACÁN ONCE WAS ONE OF THE LARGEST CITIES IN THE WORLD. BY A.D. 700, ITS POPULATION WAS BETWEEN A HUNDRED THOUSAND AND TWO HUNDRED THOUSAND PEOPLE, MORE THAN ANY GREAT CITIES IN EUROPE OF THAT TIME. THE CITY FLOURISHED IN CENTRAL MEXICO BETWEEN 200 AND 700.

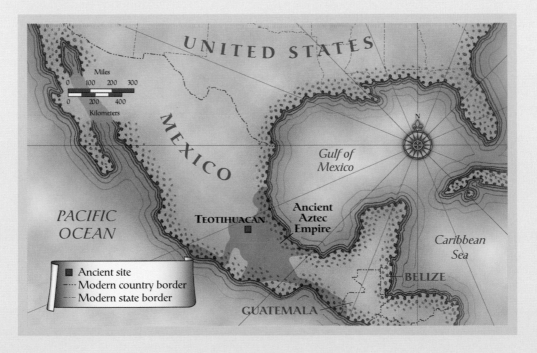

Archaeologists think that ancient tribes first settled in the area of Teotihuacán about 200 B.C. Some of these people may have been refugees from a smaller town that was destroyed by the eruption of a volcano. They soon began building a city according to a plan, with streets and buildings laid out in a gridlike pattern. Streets intersected to form neat squares.

THE CITY

The main street, was named the Avenue of the Dead. It ran between the Pyramid of the Moon and the Ciudadela, an enclosed courtyard. The Avenue of the Dead extended more than 1.5 miles (2.4 km). It ran past the Pyramid of the Sun to the Temple of the Feathered Serpent at one end of the Ciudadela.

The Avenue of the Dead, as seen from the Pyramid of the Moon. The Pyramid of the Sun is partly visible to the left of the Avenue of the Dead.

Left: *This close-up view shows one of the carvings on the Temple of the Feathered Serpent.* Right: *The carvings can be seen along the staircase of the temple. The Temple of the Feathered Serpent lies at one end of the Avenue of the Dead.*

Teotihuacán grew into ancient Mexico's first great urban area. The densely populated central city spread out into suburbs, where more people lived. In the suburbs, farmers grew the huge amounts of food needed to feed the population.

In addition to pyramids and temples, Teotihuacán had palaces for its rulers. Homes, stores, workshops, and other buildings filled the city. In these buildings, artisans made stone tools, weapons, pottery, and jewelry. They dyed yarn, made cloth, and produced other goods that city people needed.

Teotihuacán had hundreds of homes. Rulers and wealthy people lived in magnificent palaces and large homes in one part of the city. Workers lived in smaller homes in other areas. Some homes were ancient apartment buildings. Groups of families who probably were relatives lived in them. Farmers lived

EVER *Wonder?*

How do we know that the Feathered Serpent was an important ancient god?

We know it because so many different people in ancient North, South, and Central America worshipped this god. Ancient Teotihuacán had an entire temple to honor the Feathered Serpent. The ancient Maya also worshipped a feathered serpent god.

mainly in wooden houses. Other people lived in stone houses decorated with paintings and murals.

People from other parts of Mexico and Central America visited Teotihuacán. Traders came to buy and sell goods. Some may have come for religious ceremonies. Others probably visited as tourists. These visitors took ideas home with them—ideas about worshipping gods, for instance, and building pyramids. In that way, Teotihuacán influenced the ancient Maya and other civilizations in Mexico and Central America.

WONDROUS PYRAMIDS

The Pyramid of the Sun is the third-largest pyramid in the world. Archaeologists think it was built over a sacred cave that ancient people used for religious rituals.

The pyramid was built in stages starting about A.D. 100 and was completed by 225. The pyramid is actually several pyramids, one built on top of another. This amazing structure measures about 739 feet (225 m) on each of its four sides. Each side is longer than two football fields. The pyramid is 246 feet (75 m) high, almost as high as a modern twenty-five-story skyscraper.

It takes imagination to realize how beautiful the Pyramid of the Sun must have been in ancient times. Teotihuacán workers covered the sides of the pyramid with a layer of white plaster, almost like the plaster on the walls of a modern house. Archaeologists think that the sides were then painted with brilliantly colored murals, or pictures. The pictures may have included rattlesnakes, jaguars, gods, and other objects that the ancient Teotihuacán people regarded as powerful. Although the stone pyramid still remains, the plaster and paintings flaked off over the centuries.

COPYCAT *City*

The Aztec used Teotihuacán as the model for designing their capital of Tenochtitlán, located only 30 miles (48 km) away. In the Aztec language, the name meant "City of the Birth of the Gods," or "The Place Where Men Become Gods." The Aztecs believed that ancient Mexico once was a paradise inhabited by the gods and creatures who were ancestors of human beings. In the Aztec religion, the gods created and destroyed the world several times. Those gods once met at Teotihuacán to create the newest world.

"*At a place called Teotihuacán . . . the people raised pyramids for the sun and for the moon. . . . There is a hollow where they removed the stone to build the pyramids. And they built the pyramids . . . very large, just like mountains.*"

—*The Florentine Codex, twelve books about ancient Mexico written in cooperation with Aztecs under the supervision of Spanish priest Bernardino de Sahagún between 1540 and 1585*

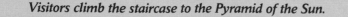

Visitors climb the staircase to the Pyramid of the Sun.

Workers probably began the Pyramid of the Moon in the first century. In recent years, archaeologists have found a burial chamber. It contained a bound, sacrificed human victim. The chamber also held rich offerings, such as figurines, mirrors, and the remains of two jaguars and two falcons.

GOOD-BYE TEOTIHUACÁN

In about 700, an unknown disaster struck this wondrous city. The pyramids, palaces, and temples in the center of the city burned. Although they were made mainly of stone, these structures had roofs and other parts made from straw, dried reeds, and wood. These materials made a hot fire. Archaeologists do not know if invaders destroyed the heart of the city or if Teotihuacán's rulers ordered its destruction. Residents of the city also may have rebelled against the rulers and set the buildings on fire in anger.

People continued to live in other parts of Teotihuacán after the destruction. Over the next two hundred years, however, people left Teotihuacán. During this time, the ancient Maya Empire in southern Mexico and Central America also was declining. People were also leaving the great Maya cities. Teotihuacán probably was a ghost town until the ancient Aztec people moved into the area about 1200. They used it as a holy place.

This mural of an Aztec priest is at Teotihuacán.

The Pyramid of the Moon sits at the end of the Avenue of the Dead in this modern photograph. Tourists walk along the avenue and among the ruins.

A MODERN WONDER

Most of ancient Teotihuacán is buried under modern Mexican towns, a military base, apartment buildings, highways, and farms. However, the pyramids and the sacred center of Teotihuacán still remain. Hundreds of thousands of visitors from around the world visit the ruins each year.

Teotihuacán is a UNESCO World Heritage Site. The Mexican people consider it a national treasure. And the Mexican government protects and preserves this wonder of the ancient world.

This illustration shows the ancient Aztec city of Tenochtitlán in central Mexico. The city was built on an island in a lake and had bridges to connect the city to the land around it.

*L*EGENDS SAY THAT PEOPLE FROM AZTLÁN, IN MODERN-DAY MEXICO, LEFT THEIR LAND TO SEARCH FOR A NEW HOME. FOR HUNDREDS OF YEARS, THEY WANDERED FROM PLACE TO PLACE LOOKING FOR A SPOT TO SETTLE DOWN AND BUILD A CITY. THESE PEOPLE BECAME KNOWN AS THE ANCIENT AZTEC, A WORD THAT MEANS "PEOPLE FROM AZTLÁN."

The Aztec's main god, Huitzilopochtli (the god of war and the sun), told them to look for a place where an eagle, perched on a cactus, was holding a snake in its beak. One day an Aztec leader looked out over Lake Texcoco in central Mexico. He could not believe his eyes. A big, prickly pear cactus stood on an island in the lake. On top of the cactus was an eagle eating a snake. In A.D. 1325, the Aztecs began building a city on that island. They named it Tenochtitlán, the Place of the Prickly Pear Cactus.

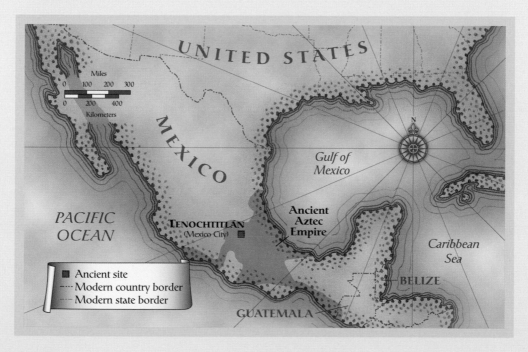

This twentieth-century painting by Miguel Covarrubias depicts the ancient city of Tenochtitlán in Mexico. The painting is at the National Museum of Anthropology in Mexico City.

As Aztec armies conquered other people in Mexico, the island-city of Tenochtitlán became the capital of a huge, powerful civilization. Aztec rulers collected taxes from the conquered people under their control. The taxes included gold, precious stones, and other valuable objects. That wealth added to the Aztec's power.

By 1500 the Aztec Empire had a population of about 15 million people in central and southern Mexico. The Aztec Empire stretched from the Pacific Ocean to the Gulf of Mexico and as far south as modern-day Guatemala. With a population of almost 200,000, Tenochtitlán was one of the world's largest cities.

CITY IN A LAKE

The Aztec were great engineers. They built an amazing system of roads connecting Tenochtitlán to other parts of their empire. Aztec armies marched to battle over the roads. Runners used the roads to carry messages from one ruler to another. Canals ran through the city like water roads. People could paddle canoes to any part of Tenochtitlán.

Causeways, or elevated roadways, connected Tenochtitlán to the mainland. The causeways had wooden bridges that allowed canoes and other boats to pass under them. The bridges could be removed at night to prevent enemies from sneaking into the city.

"We entered Tenochtitlán over a causeway that was wide enough for three or four or more horsemen to ride comfortably abreast. The causeway was built across the lake and had wooden bridges that could be raised or removed. The water was so full of canoes loaded with people who were watching us that it was frightening to see such multitudes."

—Francisco de Aguilar, a soldier in Spanish conquistador Hernán Cortés's army, ca. 1520

Many cities in Europe at that time were built in a disorganized way. The layout of streets followed no plan. Tenochtitlán was a planned city, built according to a design made in advance. The city was divided into four zones. Each zone had twenty districts. All the small side streets led into three main streets. They ran from one end of the city to the other. Each of the main streets led to one of the causeways that connected Tenochtitlán to the mainland.

Below: *This drawing of Tenochtitlán in the sixteenth century shows the setup of the streets and buildings.* **Right:** *Aztec people navigate the canals in the city in this 1890 illustration.*

Baths, Soap, Markets

Lake Texcoco's water was too salty to drink, so the Aztec built two aqueducts. These bridgelike structures had a channel on top to carry spring-fed freshwater into Tenochtitlán. Water was important for drinking, cooking, and bathing. The Aztec were a very clean people. People in Europe at this time might take one bath a year. Many Aztecs in Tenochtitlán bathed twice a day. For soap they used the root of the *copalxocotl* plant, which produced nice suds. The Aztec used the root of another plant, *tlatlauhcapatli*, to make a kind of toothpaste.

Most common people in Tenochtitlán lived in one-room houses. The people used mats of woven sticks and reeds to make their houses. They plastered the mats with mud that hardened in the sun. Wealthy people lived in brick or stone houses. These houses often had several rooms with open courtyards or patios.

With little good farmland around Tenochtitlán, the Aztec grew much of their food in artificial fields called *chinampas*. These were floating gardens built in swamps and lakes. Farmers heaped mud on huge mats made from woven reeds. Farmers grew corn, beans, chili peppers, squash, and tomatoes on chinampas.

Other people had different jobs. They made tools, weapons, cloth, baskets, jewelry, and pottery. People shopped for food and other goods in markets. Those markets sold chickens, ducks, turkeys, eggs, fruit, spices, cloth, wood, jewelry, tools, knives, and weapons, and many other goods.

This modern photo shows what is left of the chinampas south of Mexico City. The soil was constantly replenished from the bottom of the lake, so it was very fertile.

Mexican artist Diego Rivera shows the people of Tenochtitlán at the Tlatelolco market in part of a mural painted in 1945. The mural hangs at the National Palace in Mexico City.

Traders traveled to distant parts of the Aztec Empire to buy and sell cocoa beans, salt, gold ornaments, cotton, bird feathers, jaguar skins, and other goods. The Aztec had no wagons or animals to carry heavy loads. People who traveled with the traders carried everything on their backs.

Tenochtitlán's most magnificent buildings were in the center of the city. The fabulous palace of Montezuma II lay there. Montezuma II became the ruler of the Aztec Empire in 1502. His palace had one hundred rooms. It even had indoor bathrooms, which were rare in ancient times. The palace also had two zoos and saltwater and freshwater aquariums. Three hundred servants cared for the animals.

This illustration of a temple in Tenochtitlán shows people lined up outside and climbing the steps to the top of the temple. The illustration is from a book published in 1888 about the history of the United States by William Cullen Bryant and Sydney Howard Gay.

Temple-pyramids for religious worship stood nearby. These pyramids had twin staircases going up the front side. A flat area at the top held a wooden temple. The most famous was the great temple. It honored Huitzilopochtli and Tlaloc (the god of rain and fertility). The great temple had a square base about 261 feet (80 m) on each side. And the temple rose 100 feet (30 m) above the city.

Sacrificial ceremonies were held at these temples. Priests cut open a person's chest and pulled out the still-beating heart. The Aztec performed these ceremonies because of their religious beliefs. They believed that priests had to spill human blood to honor the gods. Blood was a person's most precious possession. The Aztec believed that unless humans gave that possession to the gods regularly, the world would end.

BLOOD *for the Gods*

Like other ancient people living in Mexico and Central America, the Aztec believed in sacrificing people to worship their gods. The Aztec, however, took this practice to an extreme. Legends say that in 1487, Aztec priests sacrificed more than eighty thousand prisoners of war in Tenochtitlán. The sacrifice was part of a ceremony to dedicate a temple to Huitzilopochtli.

Montezuma worried about the legend of Quetzalcoatl (above) during his reign. This image of Quetzalcoatl was created in the sixteenth century. When Hernán Cortés arrived in 1519, Montezuma thought he was the Feathered Serpent. Cortés is shown below meeting with Montezuma.

RETURN OF THE FEATHERED SERPENT

During his rule, Montezuma II worried about a legend. It warned that one of the main Aztec gods, Quetzalcoatl, the god of the sky and creation, would return to Earth and take control of the Aztec Empire. Although Quetzalcoatl meant the "Feathered Serpent," stories said this god had white skin and a black beard and would arrive from the sea.

In 1519 Montezuma thought Quetzalcoatl had arrived when Hernán Cortés and his crew landed in Mexico. Cortés was a Spanish conquistador, an explorer and conqueror. When the Spanish explorers arrived in 1519, they could not believe the city's size or beauty. Tenochtitlán reminded the Spanish of Venice, a beautiful city in Italy with many canals.

Cortés wanted to conquer the Aztec and seize their gold, jewels, and other wealth. He had an army of only about five hundred soldiers. But people who had been conquered by the Aztecs wanted their freedom back. They joined forces with Cortés.

Stories told by the conquistadors say that Montezuma felt it was hopeless to fight against Cortés. After all, he might be Quetzalcoatl. Montezuma eventually surrendered Tenochtitlán to him. This angered other leaders of Tenochtitlán. They revolted, killed Montezuma, and named a new leader to fight the Spanish.

After a long battle in which much of the city was destroyed, Cortés conquered Tenochtitlán on August 13, 1521.

Cortés's victory ended the Aztec Empire. During the next four years, the Spanish conquerors destroyed Montezuma's palace, the temple-pyramids, and the rest of Tenochtitlán. Cortés built a new city to replace this wonder of the ancient world. It became modern-day Mexico City.

A MODERN WONDER

Mexico City, one of the world's largest urban areas, sits on the buried ruins of ancient Tenochtitlán. Mexico's national symbol, almost five hundred years later, is an eagle sitting on a cactus eating a snake. It appears on the Mexican flag and on Mexican paper money.

Most of Lake Texcoco was drained to get dry land to build Mexico City. Superhighways, skyscrapers, apartment buildings, shops, and other structures cover the land where Montezuma and Cortés walked.

However, visitors still can see many remains of the Aztec Empire.

"And when we saw all those towns and villages built in the water, and other great towns on dry land, and that straight and level causeway leading to Mexico, we were astounded. These great towns . . . and buildings rising from the water, all made of stone, seemed like an enchanted vision. . . . Indeed some of our soldiers asked whether it was not all a dream. . . . It was all so wonderful that I do not know how to describe this first glimpse of things never heard of, seen, or dreamed of before."

—From The Conquest of New Spain *by Bernal Díaz del Castillo, 1632*

WONDERFUL Words

The Aztec spoke a language called Nahuatl. It was the language of native people in ancient Mexico. That language is still spoken in parts of modern-day Mexico. It lives on in modern words of Nahuatl origin. Some of those words—including chocolate, tomato, chili, coyote, avocado, and mesquite—are used in several modern languages.

Archaeologists have located the ruins of more than fifty Aztec temples. Some were discovered accidentally as workers dug the foundations for modern buildings. Archaeologists think that Mexico's main government building, the National Palace, sits on the ruins of Montezuma's palace.

Some modern-day museums have archaeological displays that show Aztec ruins. The Templo Mayor Museum displays artifacts from Tenochtitán's great temple. Legends say that the temple was built where the wandering Aztec saw the cactus, eagle, and snake.

Mexico City was built where Tenochtitlán once was. The National Palace (center) is where Montezuma's palace sat in the ancient city. Visitors to Mexico City can go to museums to see artifacts from the Aztec.

CHOOSE AN EIGHTH WONDER

Now that you've read about the seven wonders of ancient North America, do a little research to choose an eighth wonder. Or make a list with your friends, and vote to see which wonder is the favorite.

To do your research, look at some of the websites and books listed in the Further Reading and Websites section of this book. Look for places in North America that
• *have a cool history*
• *were difficult to make at the time or required new technology*
• *were extra big or tall*
• *were hidden from view or unknown for many centuries*

You might even try gathering photos and writing your own chapter on the eighth wonder!

TIMELINE

200 B.C. Archaeologists think that ancient tribes first settle in the area of Teotihuacán.

A.D. 615 Pakal comes to power and starts building Palenque into a great city.

700 Teotihuacán becomes one of the largest cities in the world with a population of a hundred thousand to two hundred thousand people.

1000 Ancient adventure stories tell of Leif Eriksson and the Vikings sailing their longships from Europe to North America.

1150 Cahokia in Illinois reaches a population of twenty thousand people, making it larger than most European cities at that time.

1325 The Aztecs begin building a city on an island in present-day Mexico, calling it Tenochtitlán.

1519 Spanish conquistador Hernán Cortés arrives in North America.

1521 Cortés conquers Tenochtitlán and conquers the inhabitants.

1840 U.S. explorers John Lloyd Stephens and Frederick Catherwood rediscover Palenque and write about the Temple of the Inscriptions.

1888 Richard Wetherill and Charlie Mason discover huge buildings nestled on the ledges of cliffs in Colorado.

1906 U.S. president Theodore Roosevelt designates the Colorado cliff area as Mesa Verde National Park.

1960 Norwegian explorer Helge Ingstad finds mysterious ruins on the eastern coast of Newfoundland, proving that Vikings visited North America before Christopher Columbus.

2006 A group of panelists for *Good Morning America* (a U.S. television show) and *USA Today* (a U.S. newspaper) choose a list of New Seven Wonders. Readers and viewers vote for an eighth wonder.

2007 NewOpenWorld Foundation, a Swiss organization, conducts a worldwide poll to choose the New Seven Wonders of the World. Results can be found at the *New 7 Wonders* website at http://www.new7wonders.com/classic/en/n7w/results/.

Glossary and Pronunciation Guide

ancient: old times, which in this book means the period up to the 1700s

archaeologists: scientists who study buildings, tools, and other remains of ancient civilizations

artifacts: statues, tools, weapons, and other objects remaining from ancient civilizations

Cahokia (kuh-HOH-kee-uh)

civilization: the way of life of a group of people, a country, or a period of time

conquistadors: Spanish soldiers who sailed to the New World for conquest and treasure

culture: the values, knowledge, and way of life of a particular group of people at a certain time

empire: lands or countries under the control of a single government or ruler

hieroglyphic: a system of writing that uses symbols to represent ideas and sounds

Haudenosaunee (HO-dee-noh-SHO-nee)

kivas (KEE-vahs)

Maya (MAH-yuh)

Mesa Verde (MAY-suh VEHR-day)

Palenque (pah-LEHNG-kay)

runes: symbols used in the written language of the ancient Vikings

Tenochtitlán (tay-nohsh-teet-LAHN)

Teotihuacán (tay-oh-tee-wah-KAHN)

UNESCO World Heritage Site: a place designated for preservation by the United Nations Educational, Scientific, and Cultural Organization because of its importance to humanity

United Nations Educational, Scientific, and Cultural Organization (UNESCO): a branch of the United Nations, an international organization devoted to cooperation among countries. UNESCO's World Heritage Centre identifies and helps protect and preserve sites that are part of the world's cultural and natural heritage.

Source Notes

11 W. C. Green, trans., "Egil's Saga," *Northvegr Foundation,* June 20, 2007, http://www.northvegr.org/lore/egils_saga/index.php (April 26, 2008).

11 Helge Ingstad and Sonya Procenko, "The Viking Connection–L'Anse aux Meadows," *Virtual Tours Newfoundland*, June 25, 2007, http://www.virtual-tours-newfoundland.ca/LanseauxMeadows/Meadows.html (April 26, 2008).

16 Constitution of the Iroquois Nations, "The Great Binding Law, Gayanashagowa," *Constitution Society*, June 14, 2007, http://www.constitution.org/cons/iroquois.htm (April 26, 2008).

19 Edward M. Chadwick, *The People of the Longhouse* (Toronto: The Church of England Publishing Co., 1897), 49.

20 Brian Cook, "Iroquois Confederacy and the Influence Thesis," June 14, 2007, http://www.Campton.sau48.k12.nh.us/iroqconf.htm (April 26, 2008).

22 Bruce E. Johansen, *Forgotten Founders* (Ipswich, MA: Gambit,1982), 56.

33 Cyrus Thomas, "The Problem of the Ohio Mounds," *Gutenberg Project*, June 25, 2007, http://www.gutenberg.org/dirs/etext03/omond10.txt (April 26, 2008).

37 Charlie Mason, "Charles Mason," *CliffDwelling.com*, June 21, 2007, http://www.cliffdwelling.com/MesaVerde/mason.htm (April 26, 2008).

38 Rose Houk, Duane A. Smith, and Faith Marcovecchio, eds., *Mesa Verde National Park: The First 100 Years* (Golden, CO: Fulcrum Publishing. 2006), 17.

41 Ibid., 16.

47 Alberto Ruz Lhuillier, quoted in "Who Is Buried in Pakal's Tomb?" *Mesoweb*, May 14, 2007, http://www.mesoweb.com/palenque/features/sarcophagus/pakals_tomb.html (April 26, 2008).

52 John Lloyd Stephens and Karl Ackerman, eds., *Incidents of Travel in Central America, Chiapas and Yucatán* (Washington, DC: Smithsonian Institution Press, 1993), 201.

59 Chris Scarre, ed., *The Seventy Wonders of the Ancient World: The Great Monuments and How They Were Built* (London: Thames & Hudson, 2000), 116.

65 Hammond Innes, *The Conquistadors* (New York: Alfred A. Knopf, 1969), 146.

70 Bernal Díaz del Castillo, *The Discovery and Conquest of New Spain*, trans. J. M. Cohen (London: Penguin Books, 1963), 214.

SELECTED BIBLIOGRAPHY

Bahn, Paul G., ed. *Cambridge Illustrated History: Archaeology*. Cambridge: Cambridge University Press, 1996.

Barcroft-Hunt, Norman. *Historical Atlas of Ancient America*. New York: Checkmark Books, 2001.

Díaz del Castillo, Bernal. *The Discovery and Conquest of New Spain*. Translated by J. M. Cohen. London: Penguin Books, 1963.

Faber, Harold. *The Discoverers of America*. New York: Charles Scribner's Sons, 1992.

Fagan, Brian. *Chaco Canyon: Archaeologists Explore the Lives of an Ancient Society*. New York: Oxford University Press, 2005.

Gomara, Francisco Lopez, de. *Cortes: The Life of the Conqueror by His Secretary*. Translated by Lesley Byrd Simpson. Berkeley: University of California Press, 1964.

Houk, Rose, Duane A. Smith, and Faith Marcovecchio, eds. *Mesa Verde National Park: The First 100 Years*. Golden, CO: Fulcrum Publishing, 2006.

Innes, Hammond. *The Conquistadors*. New York: Alfred A. Knopf, 1969.

Kopper, Philip. *The Smithsonian Book of North American Indians: Before the Coming of the Europeans*. Washington, DC: Smithsonian Books, 1986.

Mink, Claudia Gellman. *Cahokia: City of the Sun*. Collinsville, IL: Cahokia Mounds Museum Society, 1992.

Pringle, Heather. *In Search of Ancient North America*. New York: John Wiley & Co., 1996.

Scarre, Chris, ed. *The Seventy Wonders of the Ancient World: The Great Monuments and How They Were Built*. London: Thames & Hudson, 2000.

Stephens, John Lloyd, and Karl Ackerman, eds. *Incidents of Travel in Central America, Chiapas, and Yucatán*. Washington, DC: Smithsonian Institution Press, 1993.

Thomas, Cyrus. *Report on the Mound Explorations of the Bureau of Ethnology*. Washington, DC: Smithsonian Institution Press, 1985.

FURTHER READING AND WEBSITES

Books

Andryszewski, Tricia. *Walking the Earth: The History of Human Migration*. Minneapolis: Twenty-First Century Books, 2007. Human migration from prerecorded history to the present is detailed in this book. In the course of describing human movement, the book covers population, human migration, agriculture resources, and current events.

Beller, Susan Provost. *The History Puzzle: How We Know What We Know about the Past*. Minneapolis: Twenty-First Century Books, 2006. This book follows the process of fascinating detective work as historians unravel the most detailed and accurate picture of our past, including the story of Mesa Verde and the Vikings at Jellyfish Cove.

Bernstein, Josh. *Digging for the Truth*. New York: Gotham Books, 2006. This fun and informative book was written by Josh Bernstein, host of the History Channel's *Digging for the Truth* series. It has excellent information on the Vikings in North America.

Blackburn, Fred M. *The Wetherills: Friends of Mesa Verde*. Durango, CO: Durango Herald Small Press, 2006. Written to commemorate the one-hundredth anniversary of Mesa Verde becoming a national park, this book focuses on the Wetherill family. It describes Wetherill's discovery of the cliff dwellings and efforts to preserve these wonders.

Clarke, Barry. *Aztec, Inca and Maya*. New York: Dorling Kindersley, 2005. This title in the Eyewitness series provides a broad overview of the ancient Aztec, Inca, and Maya civilizations. It is loaded with pictures and information about the artifacts found at the various archaeological sites in North America.

Day, Nancy. *Your Travel Guide to Ancient Mayan Civilization*. Minneapolis: Twenty-First Century Books, 2001. Readers can become time tourists with this lively and fast-paced book that is written like a travel guide. The Passport to History series shows students what to visit, what to eat, and what to pack for trips to the ancient Mayan civilization.

Jolley, Dan. *The Hero Twins: Against the Lords of Death*. Minneapolis: Graphic Universe, 2008. The story of Hero Twins Hunter and Jaguar Deer is told in this graphic novel based on a Mayan legend. The boys are blessed with super powers and astonishing skill at a traditional Mayan ball game, but their skill soon angers the Lords of Death, rulers of the Mayan underworld.

——. *The Smoking Mountain: The Story of Popocatépetl and Iztaccíhuatl*. Minneapolis: Graphic Universe, 2009. This graphic novel tells the exciting story of the great warrior Popocatépetl. In this Aztec legend, Popocatépetl falls in love with the emperor's beautiful daughter, Iztaccíhuatl (and she with him), and endures many trials to win her.

Kops, Deborah. *Palenque*. Minneapolis: Twenty-First Century Books, 2008. This title in the Unearthing Ancient Worlds series allows readers to discover the ancient ruins at Palenque in Mexico along with the archaeologists who studied them.

Wilcox, Charlotte. *The Iroquois*. Minneapolis: Lerner Publications, 2007. Learn about the Iroquois people in this book in the Native American Histories series. The book provides a chronological history of the Iroquois tribe from its origins to modern times.

Woods, Michael, and Mary B. Woods. *Seven Wonders of Ancient Central and South America*. Minneapolis: Twenty-First Century Books, 2009. Explore wonders such as Machu Picchu in Peru and the Brazilian Stonehenge in this book detailing historic sites in Central and South America.

Wulffson, Don. *Before Columbus: Early Voyages to the Americas*. Minneapolis: Twenty-First Century Books, 2008. Archaeologists are beginning to find evidence that many European people explored North America before Columbus. Read this book to find out some of the intriguing details leading to this conclusion.

Websites

Cahokia Mounds State Historic Site
http://www.cahokiamounds.com/cahokia.html
Have an adventure visiting these amazing mounds in Illinois online. You can click on the links and visit the interpretative center and the archaeology center and learn about what the archaeologists think happened at this historic site.

Conquistadors
http://www.pbs.org/conquistadors/
This is the online companion to the PBS series on the conquistadors in South America, Central America, and parts of North America. The design of the site uses icons to move you along in learning about the conquistadors.

L'Anse aux Meadows National Historic Site of Canada
http://www.pc.gc.ca/lhn-nhs/nl/meadows/natcul/hist_e.asp
Read the story of the settlement founded by Leif Eriksson in North America. Archaeological explorations have found evidence of many different occupants of this area of Newfoundland.

Mesa Verde National Park
http://www.nps.gov/meve
Find out about the Pueblo people. Escorted by a park ranger, you can even climb to see the ancient cliff dwellings.

Mesoweb: An Exploration of Mesoamerican Cultures
http://www.mesoweb.com/
Mesoweb has a huge amount of resources about the ancient cultures of Mexico and Latin America. It specializes in information about Maya language, history, and culture and includes research articles and photographs.

World Heritage
http://whc.unesco.org/en/list
The United Nations Educational, Scientific and Cultural Organization (UNESCO) provides a list of World Heritage Sites. It includes information about Cahokia, Mesa Verde, Jellyfish Cove, and other sites.

INDEX

ABOUT THE AUTHORS

Michael Woods is a science and medical journalist in Washington, D.C., who has won many national writing awards. Mary B. Woods is a school librarian. Their previous books include the eight-volume Ancient Technology series, the Disasters Up Close series, *The History of Communication, The History of Medicine,* and *The Tomb of King Tutankhamen*. The Woodses have four children. When not writing, reading, or enjoying their grandchildren, the Woodses travel to gather material for future books.